PHILODENDRON SELLOUM

Plants grow. But the process is not quite as simple as it may seem. We had an idea, contacted experts, selected large plants, chose various locations and, last but not least, collected containers. Finally, we had all the ingredients necessary to make this book a reality. A great challenge for us, especially as so little attention has been paid to design using large plants.

Conscious of this, we elected to be creative and to try out new ideas. I would like to thank Medi for taking on that creativity, Joop for his understanding of plants and their architectural possibilities, and Dolf for his calm behind the lens. Thanks also to all those in the industry who supported us in our task.

Sander Kroll

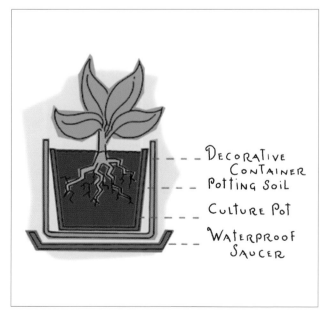

DECORATIVE CONTAINER
POTTING SOIL
CULTURE POT
WATERPROOF SAUCER

The joy of outdoor living…

From dish to designer pot…

A thumbnail sketch…

Ki Plant International - Index - Acknowledgements…

EPIPREMNUM AUREUM

FOREWORD

This marvellous book draws on two of the major threads of my life - my Dutch ancestry and a love of large tropical plants.

This English edition links what are probably the two greatest horticultural nations of Europe, the Dutch, who have taken the grower's craft to professional heights unimagined a generation ago; and the British, for whom the love of gardens and gardening led to an incomparable tradition of pioneering landscape and garden design that has evolved over more than four centuries. A passion that, if anything, burns stronger today than ever before.

The magnificent photographs that illustrate this book provide an elegant essay in nature as art. They explore the breathtaking range of architectural form, shape and pattern available from the tropical plant palette. From ultra-modern "cool" to explosive "jungle", plants can transform the mood and texture of the humblest cottage or grey office into something special.

I love these plants. The fact that they originally came to our shores from some of the most exotic locations in the world is grist to every dreamer's mill and just adds to their mystique. That so many of them can, with a little tender care, adapt to the conditions found in our homes and places of work should fire the imagination of designers everywhere to "think plants" and so encourage the public's understanding of the importance of plants.

Unfortunately my old Cornish farmhouse is completely unsuited to tropical plants, being both cold and dark. However, life does have its little compensations and my work at the Eden Project gives me possibly the widest range of exotic plants in Europe to drool over. I am delighted to recommend this book to anyone with the salsa pulse in their veins and ambitions to become "green-fingered" with attitude. On the other hand for those who haven't yet caught the bug, maybe it should be offered on prescription.

Tim Smit
Co-Founder of The Eden Project
Restorer of the Lost Gardens of Heligan

MONSTERA DELICIOSA

Ambience in every interior ...

There is more to life than work. Reading a magazine on a day off, or enjoying a relaxed weekend breakfast in congenial company are moments when we realise just how wonderful life is.

To cope with the hectic pace of modern life, we long for peace and tranquillity. Home has never been more important. So it is essential that our living environment be designed with care so that we can enjoy every moment of the day. Interior decoration offers a lasting source of pleasure, in which creativity coupled with audacity can produce extraordinary results.

One of the best ways of giving any interior a peaceful atmosphere is by using large plants. They give a sense of calm, and seem to make one dream of far away places. Large plants create ambience and put the finishing touch to any interior. They complete the living environment. Whether a romantic or business-like effect is required, bringing green plants indoors makes it all possible.

Selecting a large plant is a serious business and involves commitment. Silent though they may be, plants make demands, which must be met. Their care and maintenance requires sensitivity and awareness of their needs. The relationship with a plant, however, is not for ever. The time may come for a change of décor. This may require a new plant or perhaps just a new pot for a familiar friend.

The innovative and professional way in which large plants are presented in this book offers a wealth of new ideas for interior design. Enjoy this wonderful variety and take up the challenge. Bring large plants indoors.

FICUS ELASTICA 'DECORA'

Modern with a dash of nostalgia. The warm
green of Ficus elastica 'Decora' contrasts
beautifully with the cool shades of the room.
This stocky plant with thick leaves has made a
comeback. It offers a lively, contrasting element in
a modern interior.

PHOENIX ROEBELENII

A miraculous day. Even the spacious interior appears in a new light: transparent and warm.

The Far East seems near. Time is unimportant. The allure of this graceful Phoenix roebelenii is endless.

MUSA 'PURPLE RAIN'

The robust leaves of this red Musa have a
unique radiance. The plant creates an exotic
atmosphere in this airy living environment.
Plenty of space is required, as this special variety
of the banana family needs room to grow.

SIMPLY BEAUTIFUL ...

The very simplicity of these containers gives the
effect of size. It is almost as if they know that
nothing elaborate is needed. They are the perfect
complement for this exceptional Musa. After all,
opposites attract.

SCHEFFLERA ARBORICOLA

JOHANNESTEIJSMANNIA

Bring life into the home with the light, dancing movement of

Schefflera arboricola. Its frivolous, nonchalant character softens

austerity. Its spread makes this plant a lively addition to any

interior. It will remain so as long as it has good light.

'Altifrons'

Licuala grandis

This stately, exotic beauty makes one yearn for warm summer

evenings. This plant combines strength and fragility. Just as

they do in the wild, the leaves of Licuala grandis sometimes

form brown edges. This dignified plant blends perfectly into

its surroundings.

BAMBUSA VULGARIS 'VITTATA'

The interior space is large and light. The most important function is fulfilled by a single plant, Bambusa vulgaris 'Vittata'. Its sole purpose is to be beautiful. And although the plant may shed a leaf from time to time, it will give you intense pleasure. This Bambusa needs plenty of water in the summertime.

In these hectic times, people long for peace and security, the chance to stop and think about the important things in life. The mysterious Bambusa ventricosa with its fascinating stem contributes to this relaxing atmosphere.

BAMBUSA VENTRICOSA

FICUS BINNENDIJKII 'ALII'

Playing with shape, line and colour. Ficus binnendijkii 'Alii' gives a natural look to the interior. This tropical plant is eye-catching, particularly its intriguing stem, often festooned with aerial roots.

PACHIRA AQUATICA

A real strong man, the Pachira aquatica hails from South
America. This hardy plant can thrive almost anywhere.
With its stylishly braided trunk, it would enhance any
room in the house.

Cissus capensis

Placed in the entrance hall, this plant catches the first rays of sunshine
in early spring. There this Cissus capensis gives a warm welcome to
visitors. A plant of robust appearance, but gentle character, this
member of the grape family craves warmth and attention. Regular
trimming establishes a rapport between man and plant.

CARYOTA MITIS

Looking at Caryota mitis is an endless adventure. It is permanently exotic. The leaves are characterised by their rugged and capricious structure. So it is no surprise to find that this fast-growing plant is also known as the 'Fishtail Palm'.

DRACAENA 'COMPACTA'

Nothing to do. Sheer enjoyment of a beautiful day in the company of an easy-going plant. Dracaena

'Compacta' completes this picture of idleness. It is a mother plant, among the hardiest in the world,

thriving even in places where little light can penetrate.

Cycas revoluta

If you would like to bring a touch of the tropics home, you will fall for Cycas revoluta. A unique looking plant of character: symmetrical and compact. From the moment the plant moves in with you, it will reign over your interior.

Dracaena surculosa

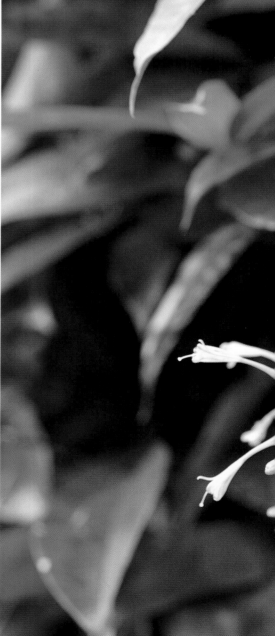

Zamioculcas zamiifolia

Sturdy, robust leaves that gleam like the most precious pearls. No wonder Zamioculcas zamiifolia has so many admirers. Its beauty is captivating. Originally from Madagascar, this plant is particularly prized for its decorative growth.

PHILODENDRON SELLOUM

A highly imaginative combination. This huge, egg-shaped container shows off the many-leaved

Philodendron selloum to perfection. Together the ceramic pot and plant creates a whole, in complete

harmony with the light surroundings.

Schefflera actinophylla 'Amate'

This Schefflera actinophylla 'Amate' stands proudly in the living room. It can reach heights of thirty

metres outdoors, but this umbrella tree of Indonesian extraction knows its limits indoors. Its distinct,

hand-shaped leaves add a touch of solidity to the interior.

SANSEVIERIA TRIFASCIATA 'LAURENTII'

Sansevieria is strong, hardy and definitely the easiest of plants to care for. Combine this classic lady with a modern cylindrical container and it looks particularly smart, especially on the windowsill. It brings the feeling of days gone by to a modern interior.

Anthurium

The natural world is an inexhaustible source of inspiration for the layout of every room in the house. Large plants in the conservatory offer a dazzling variety of green shades set against the vegetation outside. It soon becomes clear just how the different species of plant alter the atmosphere in a home.

Tettrastigma voinierianum

A room is changed when a plant is brought in. Anthurium lends itself to

romantic moments. It is a subtle and seductive plant with sensuous, rounded,

crimson flowers. Tetrastigma is a nimble plant. Although its leaves climb

playfully upwards, it brings peace to the room.

ANTHURIUM

Tetrastigma voinierianum

A glorious explosion of green by the window. Asparagus falcatus is a mass of innumerable fine leaves. This plant grows equally well in traditional potting soil or in hydro-culture. It perfects the living environment. A prominent position with plenty of sunlight will bring out the best in the plant.

The matchless beauty, elegance and strength of the Howea, better known as the Kentia palm, are undisputed. This palm originates from Lord Howe Island, Australia, and has enjoyed years of immense popularity. It flourishes in a dry atmosphere, even in low light and with minimal care and attention. There is a wide range of sizes to choose from.

HOWEA FORSTERIANA

FICUS LYRATA

This pair of green, stately plants welcome you into the house. They bring a peaceful atmosphere to the

entrance and a touch of nostalgia for days gone by. This effect is enhanced by the dark, cone-shaped pots.

They are a wonderful contrast to the rough, leathery leaves.

True beauty comes from within. This shaggy Cyperus papyrus looks proudly out into the daylight, while its

slender stems stand deep in water. A native of Egypt, Cyperus has been made into paper since 2750 BC.

Usefulness and beauty going hand in hand.

CYPERUS PAPYRUS

Styles from different cultures blend in this room. The Dracaena provides a colourful accent and not for nothing has it earned its nickname of 'Yellow Stripe'. The plant looks artistically decorated with sword-like leaves striped in shades of green, white and lime.

DRACAENA 'YELLOW STRIPE'

Dreaming in a warm bath. Happy, romantic memories fill your thoughts, inspired by the Alocasia x amazonica's heart-shaped contours. It is strong but with a gentle side. A plant of contradictions, like a woman. Its message is love.

ALOCASIA X AMAZONICA

PHOENIX ROEBELENII

Get to know the different faces of this impressive Phoenix

roebelenii. With its graceful branches, it fits in anywhere.

Whether in the midst of a richly decorated room or in a

plain office, this prolific and hardy palm from the Far East

always looks right.

PANDANUS UTILIS

Studying this Pandanus utilis is a never-ending adventure. It is found on the beaches of Madagascar. Its growth pattern is most unusual. The branches wind their way upwards like a screw. But be careful. Attractive though the red edges may look, touching them will reveal the plant's prickly side.

YUCCA ELEPHANTIPES

One of the best-known jewels in the Mexican treasure-trove of plants, it comes into its own in a terracotta pot. Its solid character and distinctive stem, and the wide range of varieties available, make this Yucca elephantipes the ideal choice for any interior.

CHRYSALIDOCARPUS LUTESCENS

AGLAONEMA 'MARY ANN'

Epipremnum Aureum

POLYSCIAS FRUTICOSA

A feeling of peace, hope and harmony permeates the room. Time is irrelevant. Only the beauty of this Polyscias matters. Its delicate leaves and branches are much admired. Refined, exceptional, remarkably like a bonsai in its shape.

BEAUCARNEA RECURVATA

Experience the lightness of being. In this oasis of calm there is an intriguing interaction. Horizontal, vertical and diagonal lines create balance in the open space.

Beaucarnea recurvata from Mexico, robust and yet frivolous, accentuates this effect.

DRACAENA REFLEXA 'SONG OF INDIA'

A joy to behold, an exceptionally beautiful plant. Not quite as lush green as other

Dracaena varieties, this 'Song of India' often shows wood through the foliage. It almost

seems to radiate light.

DRACAENA REFLEXA 'SONG OF JAMAICA'

Timeless elegance. A mood of pure languor hangs in the air. Dracaena reflexa

'Song of Jamaica' has a strong but not over-dominant presence. It is a long-living

plant. With cosy indoor warmth, it thrives as happily as in its natural environment.

Ficus benjamina 'Exotica'

MEDINILLA MAGNIFICA

Eye-catching, seductive, graceful. Medinilla magnifica is an enchantress. Its feminine shape and lovely floral accents make it a jewel among flowering plants. No wonder that Medinella, the Art Director of this book, was named after this plant.

COCOS NUCIFERA

The exotic need not be expensive! Cocos nucifera proves the point. One of the
cheapest varieties, it fills the living environment with green in a way that few plants
can rival. The effect is enhanced by its long leaves, which grow directly out of the
coconut itself.

Dracaena fragrans 'Massangeana'

Cheerful, colourful furniture injects a holiday feeling into the home. With Dracaena fragrans 'Massangeana' the playful atmosphere is enhanced. This plant happily takes centre-stage. It completes the room's design.

DRACAENA — 'WARNECKEI'

— 'LEMON LIME'

— 'JANET CRAIG'

MASCARENA

LAGENICAULUS

Create an indoor garden effect with these variegated and green Dracaena deremensis

plants. The line of three differently coloured yet related plants harmonise, forming a whole.

They contrast beautifully with the pale background.

DRACAENA MARGINATA 'BICOLOR'

This little ruffian reminds one of the exquisite colours of autumn. Striving for perfection,

this Dracaena simultaneously develops leaves of reddish brown and yellow green, hence

the name 'Bicolor'. In this wicker basket it is the centre of attention.

ECHINOCACTUS GRUSONII

FEROCACTUS TOWNSENDIANUS

Anyone who likes cactus plants will definitely fall for this Ferocactus. With its fiery, exceptionally

strong hooks, this plant is the epitome of insolence. It is nobody's fool and looks good in a terracotta

bowl.

The contrast between large and small is a prominent feature of modern interior design. The

Echinocactus grusonii suits this perfectly. Its lovely round form, which can grow to a maximum

diameter of 120 cm, is shown at its best in an oversized container.

PACHYCEREUS PRINGLEI

MUSA NANA

Decorative and functional ...

A quite different, more natural atmosphere in the office. Not new desks, chairs or computers, but large, imposing plants. They create an ambience all their own in any setting. Nowadays in many European countries, design of the workplace without large interior plants would be unthinkable. Many architects now make provisions for plants in their designs. Not only for aesthetic reasons, but also because plants have beneficial effects.

Is there anyone who doesn't feel a sense of peace in nature? Large plants alleviate the tension of the modern age. Our diaries are full. We dash from meeting to meeting. The stress factor is high. Large plants give us the opportunity to stop and reflect. It's not surprising that research has shown the calming, positive effect they have on the working environment. Stress is reduced and productivity increased. Just looking at large plants gives one a feeling of relaxation and well-being.

What is more, plants help to create a healthy working environment. They increase the humidity in a dry office and purify the air of toxic substances such as formaldehyde. We are becoming increasingly aware of the beneficial effects of plants in the workplace. Several prominent hospitals are already using plants in their interior design.

Overseas and domestic producers of large plants have responded well to the demand for material destined for large offices and company facilities. The range has expanded considerably to include varieties which can grow in low light or where climatic conditions are poor. The following pages show numerous glorious examples of what is currently possible.

CODIAEUM

Asian 'blood' courses through the veins of this capricious plant. Codiaeum, also known as Croton, is never dull. There seems to be new growth every time one looks. Its branches are set off perfectly by these solid aluminium containers, themselves a wonderful contrast to the mocha-coloured background.

Dizygotheca elegantissima

Simplicity and charm combine. The container is stark, the russet leaves elegant. Place Dizygotheca elegantissima in a sunny spot and watch its unique growth pattern. As it grows taller, the plant will develop ever-larger and increasingly coarse leaves at the crown.

WASHINGTONIA ROBUSTA

64

Imposing and compelling. Washingtonia robusta is a natural focus of attention. It is as if we have woken in another world, where people have shrunk to tiny beings and plants have attained overwhelming heights. This giant's leaves alone can reach a diameter of one and a half metres!

PANDANUS UTILIS

Pandanus utilis adds a dash of exclusivity to a room. This fresh, verdant Screw Palm with its bristly red edges is most unusual. It needs space to grow. There is plenty of that where it comes from, the coast of Madagascar.

PODOCARPUS LATIFOLIUS 'MAKI'

PODOCARPUS LATIFOLIUS 'MAKI'

It is not surprising that the Podocarpus has been seen more often in recent years. Its long, dark leaves fill the room with an intense

green. Its compact shape makes it an exquisite addition to any interior. It is impressive alone in an entrance-hall and looks radiant in a

busy area. It never loses its individuality.

RHAPIS EXCELSA

A combination of strong lines with a certain frivolity. The furniture is
simple and the plant's deep green, hand-shaped leaves add a lighter
touch. Rhapis excelsa has been a favourite for years. It looks good in
any interior and is a strong survivor.

FICUS MICROCARPA 'COMPACTA'

Simplicity itself. An interior where the balance of colours takes

centre stage. Two plants in the line of vision with some brightly

coloured chairs. In the foreground, Ficus 'Compacta', a native of

Malaysia. Its natural shape is set off by the blue synthetic container.

Ficus microcarpa 'Green Gem'

PHOENIX ROEBELENII

Bring life into the entrance-hall with an imposing Phoenix roebelenii,

ensconced in a stunning pot. The clear blue of the pot picks up the

shades of azure in the paintings on the wall. Visitors will return to enjoy

this attractive arrangement.

FICUS MICROCARPA

In the midst of the daily round where work
sets the pace, this stylish Ficus microcarpa with
its deep verdant leaves gives a much-needed
sense of peace. Modest, not dominating.
A relaxing way to begin a presentation.

FICUS BENJAMINA 'PEEL KROON'

A visitor relaxes dreamily in the red chair. The simple,

remarkable beauty of this special bonsai-shaped Ficus is

the focus of attention. A well-chosen feature in the stark,

grey interior.

STRELITZIA NICOLAI

POLASKIA CHICHIPE

A waiting-room for pampered guests. A powerful decor. The steel walls seem lighter in shades of blue, terracotta and green. Requiring little care and attention Polaskia chichipe gives maximum effect for minimal effort.

VEITCHIA MERRILLII

A spacious interior demands an impressive decor. Veitchia merrillii is a splendid choice. The five-metre plants dominate the environment. Rooted in the ground, they are truly part of their surroundings. They are the focal point of the whole design.

OLEA EUROPAEA

The way the light falls on this Olea europaea transforms the area into a delightful place to unwind. Our thoughts wander as we gaze at the weather-beaten trunk, and we are brought down to earth by the huge terracotta pot.

YUCCA ROSTRATA

This composition shows how less can be more. A few simple but stunning ingredients. The graceful lines of the stairway blend in to those of the metalic pot. The colours of the Yucca rostrata do the rest.

Ficus benjamina 'Exotica'

Ficus is an ideal choice for the office. Its striking open braided trunk stands out particularly well next to simple furniture and plain office accessories. The matching container links the plant to its surroundings.

Yucca elephantipes

Not to be forgotten is this robust, hardy Yucca elephantipes. It is one of the most popular plants

for the working environment and scores high marks for its beauty too.

The meeting is over. It is time to go home and get on with other things. Only Beaucarnea recurvata stays behind. It is a faithful partner, holding the fort and welcoming you the next day with open arms.

BEAUCARNEA RECURVATA

CITROFORTUNELLA MICROCARPA

A gentle light is reflected on creamy white and terracotta tiles. A visitor strides through the hallway. The pattern seems reassuring. It is a perfectly balanced interior. The right colours, the best light and the perfect plant.

FICUS BENJAMINA 'EXOTICA',
BOUGAINVILLEA, CITROFORTUNELLA

Take a break from the daily grind. Enjoy a few moments of relaxation. Alone or with a colleague. This natural environment

creates the perfect mood. The different plant types create a cosy atmosphere despite the vast size of the area. Then

revitalised, make a fresh start.

FICUS BENJAMINA 'DANIELLE'

FICUS BENJAMINA 'EXOTICA'

PHYLLOSTACHYS AUREA

THE JOY OF OUTDOOR LIVING ...

The terrace is looking its best. We have time to make the most of it. Each season has its own charm. On sultry summer evenings we can relax with friends until the early hours. Or just listen to the rustling of the breeze. The glorious colours of autumn never pall. They reinvigorate us for the winter. As the first rays of sunlight announce the coming of spring, we look forward to a new year.

Interest in patio and garden design is on the increase. This reflects the way we live today. We need more space and less constraint. We like the freedom of living outside.

Plants transform the garden, conservatory, patio and veranda. They create atmosphere. Adventurous, exotic, calming or stimulating, plants set the mood. They can transform the porch as well. Two identical plants in simple yet imposing pots give a regal touch. A splendid greeting from Mother Nature.

There are recognisable trends in outdoor plants. But Buxus is a permanent favourite. For years, gardeners and architects have been inspired by its versatility. It can be shaped into any number of surprisingly different shapes. No terrace is complete without one.

CHAMAEROPS HUMILIS

Exuberant yet modest. The frivolous hand-
shaped leaves are softened by greyish green
tones. Strong and compact, Chamaerops humilis
gives this terrace a Mediterranean feel.

Murraya paniculata

A distinctive composition of place, plant and pot. The
striking Murraya paniculata plants are a perfect match for
the lines of the pots in this cool, quiet spot. See how well
the two go together. In the spring, the scent of the creamy
white flowers makes one long for summer days.

OLEA EUROPAEA

Sultry summer evenings. The Mediterranean beckons as
the olive tree reveals its fruit. Olea europaea cannot have
too much sunshine. A terracotta pot brings out the best in
this popular tree.

METROSIDEROS

The rich profusion of colour on this patio is intoxicating.
Silvery green leaves and flamboyant red flowers of
Metrosideros look wonderful in a terracotta pot. The
finishing touch is to place it next to an olive tree.

BOUGAINVILLEA GLABRA

With its distinctive trunk, Bougainvillea glabra is a unique plant. It loves summer on the terrace and is endlessly

versatile, with 'flowers' in so many glorious colours. Remember to protect it from the harsh cold of winter.

The evergreen Buxus is an eye-catcher and enhances any location. For centuries, it has inspired gardeners and architects in its own special way. It can still surprise us by the many different shapes it can assume. There is good reason for its renewed popularity, its great versatility is much appreciated by the discerning buyer. Recently Buxus has become the most popular of all evergreen patio plants.

Buxus

Grand and awe-inspiring? Modest and refined? Soft and voluptuous? Anything is possible with Buxus. By trimming it into a playful ball or shaping it into a startling pyramid, a completely different look can be created. Buxus looks good, whether in a terracotta pot or a steel container. It can also be planted in a wicker basket and is even happy growing in the ground.

Buxus can set the scene in any environment without losing its own identity. All it needs is an annual trim. In fact, Buxus is indispensable, on any patio, in any garden.

MUSA NANA

Feel the scorching temperatures and the sultry heat. This familiar,

fast growing Musa brings the tropics a bit closer to home. Its great

leaves do require space however, space and light.

A sun-filled patio, a spacious veranda, a large conservatory or a

light, airy room are places where this plant feels most at home.

PITTOSPORUM TOBIRA
'NANA'

FICUS CARICA

The subtle designs on the pot accentuate the fine, glossy leaves of Pittosporum tobira 'Nana'. Although compact in growth, it spreads in width. Any patio would gain from such pleasant and modest company, particularly in the spring when its lovely white flowers bloom. Remember to protect it against the frost.

PITTOSPORUM TOBIRA 'NANA'

FROM DISH TO DESIGNER POT ...

The pot complements the plant. The wrong choice can spoil the look of the plant. Fortunately, the possibilities are endless. Garden centres, florists and interior landscapers offer a wide range of containers in all shapes, sizes and materials to suit any plant, style or location.

There was a time when containers were almost irrelevant. We were happy just putting a saucer underneath the plastic pot provided by the shop. But as more attention was paid to interior design, the pot took on a new role. We realised that plants were enhanced by the right container and that pots added an important extra touch to the interior.

Manufacturers have responded creatively. Nowadays, there is a pot to suit every style, taste and price-range. From a modern classic to a plain, functional container, anything is possible. Pots can transform a room, completely changing the atmosphere. Terracotta lends a Mediterranean feel, ceramics a touch of the Far East while aluminium suits a professional interior.

Pots are now the province of designers. There is a wealth of exciting new ideas. Contemporary trends are reflected in style and colour. Contrasts, dark and light, large and small. A modern look is achieved by planting a ball-shaped cactus in an oversized pot (see page 56). Simplicity is the key. However, the pot should not be the main focus of attention. The simple lines of a contemporary container bring out the best in a lush plant.

TERRACOTTA

Timeless beauty. Terracotta has enchanted us for centuries. Its colour is determined by the local clay, from the sea or river. Greek pots tend to be pale grey, Italian ones more salmon coloured. Terracotta is lightly porous, so some waterproofing is needed indoors.

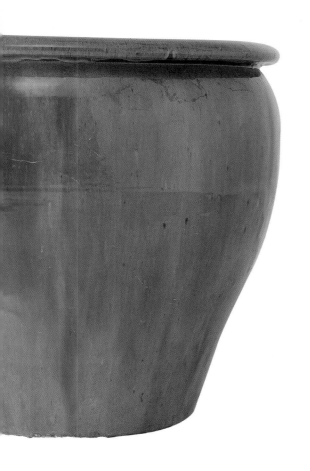

CERAMICS

Traditional stoneware and ceramic pots are ever-popular. Handmade and unique, or perfected by machine, the choice is yours. Used indoors, handmade pots need a saucer.

Natural materials

Wicker baskets and wooden containers have a natural beauty. They are perfect for plants. In the garden, they blend into the surrounding greenery. Indoors, they add an attractive, rustic touch. Lining them avoids leaks.

ALUMINIUM AND STAINLESS STEEL

Containers of aluminium and stainless steel are really eye-catching. Durable and versatile, they come in a

matte, brushed or polished finish. Prefer a pattern? No problem! They come in all shapes and sizes, with

or without castors. Some are quite expensive, perfect for the business environment, yet they also look

good in an antique setting.

SYNTHETIC

Simple, efficient and beautiful. Polyester and PVC pots have become firm favourites.

Unlike the more natural pots, they don't allow a single drop of water to escape. There is a

vast range of colours and sizes to choose from. Manufacturers are guided by contemporary

trends in interior design, such as the contrast between light and dark.

LARGE PLANTS... BEHIND THE SCENES

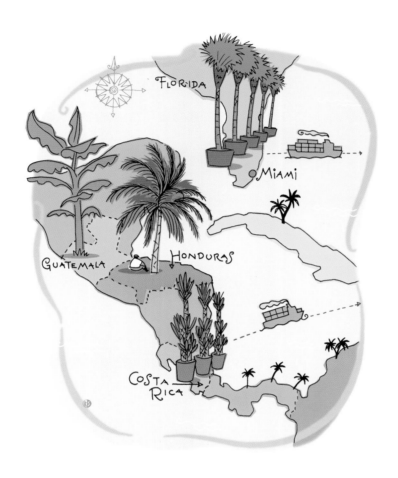

Origins

The large tropical plants seen in Europe come from countries with warm climates all over the world. Some

seeds arrived washed up by the sea, although more often they were discovered by explorers and curious plant

hunters. Along with other exotic treasures, these travellers would bring back seeds and cuttings of all kinds of

fascinating plants to be planted back home to see what would take and reproduce. In time it became clear

that growing plants in greenhouses at home was not the only option. Many tropical countries offered excellent

opportunities for the rapid production of plants.

Production

Central America is one such region. Millions of plants are grown here. It's not surprising as the soil and climate are perfect for fast all year round production. In recent years, production has taken off in places such as Costa Rica in the south and Florida in the north. The export of large plants was practically unheard of only three decades ago when growers produced primarily for a local market. Large plants were just seen as decorative additions to the garden or patio. All this changed with increasing sea and air transport to North America and Europe. There, people were delighted to bring

a touch of the tropics indoors. The large plant as an interior asset was born.

Inspection

Many plants imported into Europe come from nurseries in Central America and Florida. Southern Florida is one of the largest suppliers. Contrary to what many people believe, nothing is taken from nature itself. That was occasionally the case long ago, but nowadays the rules have been tightened and are strictly enforced. Inspection is a major part of the whole process of production and export. Prior to export, rigorous tests are carried out to establish quality and correct identification. The local phyto-pathologist checks plants for disease and deals with any problems which may adversely affect the quality of the product. Soil samples are sometimes taken. When a shipment of plants is approved, it receives the necessary certificate and clean bill of health required by the large plant export trade. On arrival in Europe, the plants also undergo extensive inspection to check for any imported diseases or insects.

Transport

It is well known that plants are sensitive to long-distance transport. Journeys range from two days up to as long as three weeks. The risk of damage to the plants is high. So producers and exporters take various measures to protect the plants from quality loss. Plants are carefully packed and the cargo area is fitted with air conditioning and heating equipment. The humidity can also be controlled. Smaller, more delicate varieties are usually transported by air as they cannot be kept in dark conditions for too long. Larger plants, from one and a half metres up to twelve meters are more resilient. They can be sealed in refrigerated containers and exported by sea. The temperature in the container is maintained at a constant level.

On arrival

When a large plant arrives in Europe, it needs to become acclimatised to its new environment. It cannot go straight into a living room. First it is kept in a nursery for a specific period of time. Climate and conditions here are completely different from those of the land of its origin. In fact measures are also taken prior to export, which enable the plants to adapt to the conditions of their future home. Palm and Ficus trees from Florida, for instance, are kept in 'open shade houses' before being shipped. These structures, with dark nylon ceilings, get the plants accustomed to a lower light.

New soil is a stimulus for new growth. Growers repot the plants on arrival. New roots and leaves should then develop. The acclimatisation period in the nursery can vary between one and eight months. Only then is the plant stable and ready for sale.

Supply and product range

The range of large plants has sharply increased in the last thirty years. This is a result of new cultivation, packing and shipment techniques as well as increased demand for more exclusive plants. New varieties constantly appear on the market. Fifteen years ago, a Ficus with a braided stem was unimaginable, today it is a common sight in many interiors. There has been a vast increase in the number of plants suitable for low light conditions. Central American and Asian countries have also responded to demand. Plants such as Rhapis excelsa (see page 68) with its beautiful, hand-shaped leaves; Dracaena reflexa (see pages 48 — 49) with its intriguing stems; and Ficus benjamina 'Danielle' (see page 90) with its compact style of growth and intense, deep green leaves are just a few of the choices available.

CARE AND MAINTENANCE ...

There are many ways to care for plants. They can simply be placed on a saucer in their original pot or in a larger watertight container. However, other methods of maintenance offer various advantages. Hydroculture and semi-hydro systems save time and effort. Watering once every two to four weeks is sufficient. Nutrients can be given at the same time. What is more, with these systems the plant develops a healthy root formation.

The majority of large plants available are grown in soil. But many are also available in hydroculture. Instead of soil, these plants are re-rooted in a pot filled with granules of expanded clay. In this chapter care and maintenance methods are described for plants in soil (soil system and semi-hydro) and plants in leca (hydroculture).

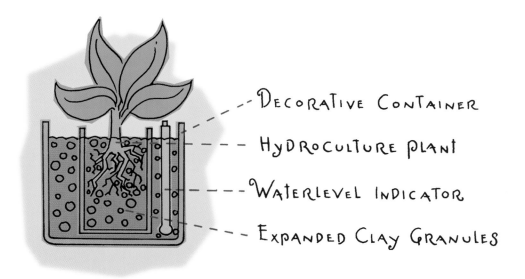

DECORATIVE CONTAINER

HYDROCULTURE PLANT

WATERLEVEL INDICATOR

EXPANDED CLAY GRANULES

Hydroculture

Using this method, specially grown plants are placed in a pot filled only with expanded clay granules. There is no soil at all. The roots grow between the granules, which secure the plant. There is plenty of room for water around the clay, so that one watering per month is usually sufficient. Controlling the level of water in the reservoir is easy using the waterlevel indicator. Although widely popular in Europe, hydroculture is rarely used in the UK.

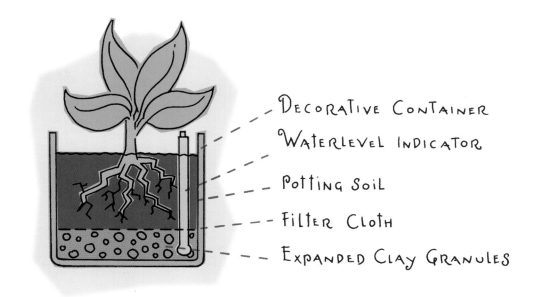

Decorative Container
Waterlevel Indicator
Potting Soil
Filter Cloth
Expanded Clay Granules

Semi-hydro method

This irrigation method combines aspects of soil and hydroculture. The plants are in soil. A reservoir of expanded

clay granules is made at the bottom of the pot. The reservoir is separated from the soil using a porous cloth. The

root growth penetrates the cloth, allowing the plant to derive its nutrients not only from the soil, but also from

the water at the bottom. The waterlevel meter indicates how much water is left in the reservoir.

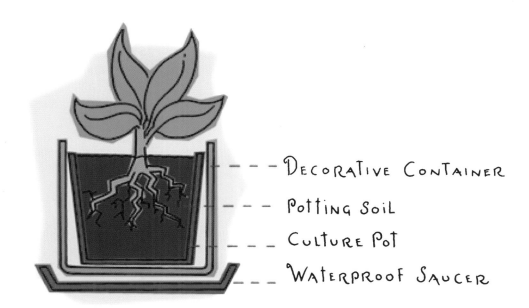

Decorative Container
Potting Soil
Culture Pot
Waterproof Saucer

Soil culture method

With this simple method the plant grows in soil in a watertight pot. The plant has no water reservoir and so

needs to be watered at least once a week. Too much or too little water has an immediate effect on the

growth and the quality of the plant.

A Thumbail sketch ...

Our aim has been to create a book which can also serve as a reference. This section includes the names and photos of the plants mentioned in the preceding chapters, as well as some extra examples.

This thumbnail sketch gives precise information regarding lighting requirements, potential plant height and the various styles of growth. A clear explanation of the icons used is set out on the page opposite. The page number is given for plants illustrated in this book. Plants are shown next to a chair to indicate their height.

All the plants in this overview are available from specialist suppliers or through the interior landscapers listed in this book. They will explain what is possible, the nutrients required, and the type of growing method best suited to the plants.

LEGEND

Recommended light level:

direct sunlight

no direct sunlight

shade

Height:

in cm

Growth forms available:

flowering

shrub form

'touffe'

branched

single stem

multi-stem

moss pole

climbing/hanging plant

straight stem

braided stem

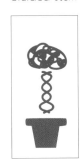

spiral stem

open braid

Foliage plants

Aglaonema
Chinese evergreen

see page 42

30-70 cm

Alocasia amazonica

see page 39

50-150 cm

Asparagus falcatus

see page 34

30-150 cm

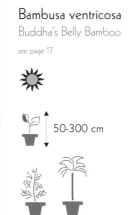

Bambusa ventricosa
Buddha's Belly Bamboo

see page 17

50-300 cm

Bambusa vulgaris 'Vittata'

see page 16

50-600 cm

Beaucarnea recurvata
Nolina, Ponytail palm

see pages 47, 86, 87

50-300 cm

Caryota mitis
Fishtail palm

see page 22

Chamaedorea seifrizii
Bamboo palm

50-800 cm

125-200 cm

Chrysalidocarpus lutescens
Areca, Golden cane palm

see page 42

100-600 cm

Cissus capensis
Grape ivy

see page 20

150-200 cm

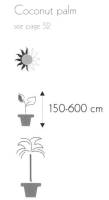

Cocos nucifera
Coconut palm
see page 52

150-600 cm

Codiaeum
Croton
see page 62

100-200 cm

Cycas revoluta
Sago palm, Cycad

see page 24

30-400 cm

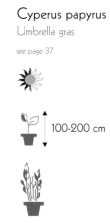

Cyperus papyrus
Umbrella gras

see page 37

100-200 cm

Dizygotheca elegantissima
False aralia

see page 63

100-400 cm

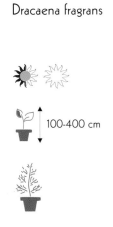

Dracaena fragrans

100-400 cm

Dracaena fragrans 'Compacta'

see page 23

100-160 cm

Dracaena fragrans 'Janet Craig'

see page 54

100-200 cm

Dracaena fragrans 'Lemon Lime'

see page 54

 100-220 cm

Dracaena fragrans 'Massangeana'

see page 53

 100-300 cm

Dracaena fragrans 'Steudneri'

 70-200 cm

Dracaena marginata

 80-400 cm

Dracaena reflexa 'Song of India'
Pleomele 'Song of India'
see page 48

 80-400 cm

Dracaena reflexa 'Song of Jamaica'
Pleomele 'Song of Jamaica'
see page 49

 80-400 cm

Epipremnum aureum
Scindapsus aureus, Devil's ivy
see page 43

40-300 cm

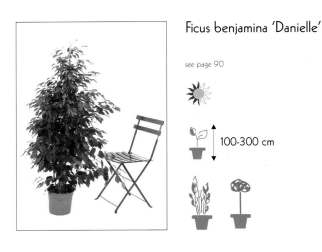

Ficus benjamina 'Danielle'
see page 90

100-300 cm

Ficus benjamina 'Exotica'
Weeping fig
see pages 50, 84, 89, 91

50-1000 cm

Ficus binnendijkii 'Alii'
see page 18

60-500 cm

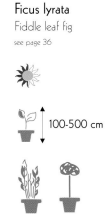

Ficus lyrata
Fiddle leaf fig
see page 36

100-500 cm

Ficus microcarpa
Ficus nitida
see page 74

100-600 cm

Howea forsteriana
Kentia palm

see page 35

60-500 cm

Licuala grandis
Ruffled wax palm

see page 15

80-250 cm

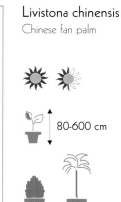

Livistona chinensis
Chinese fan palm

80-600 cm

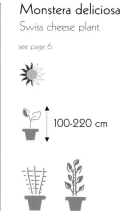

Monstera deliciosa
Swiss cheese plant

see page 6

100-220 cm

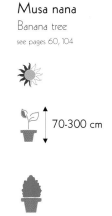

Musa nana
Banana tree

see pages 60, 104

70-300 cm

Pachira aquatica

see page 19

50-250 cm

Philodendron selloum

see page 26

  80-200 cm

Phoenix canariensis
Canary date palm

  80-400 cm

Phoenix roebelenii
Pygmy date palm

see pages 10, 40, 73

  80-400 cm

Podocarpus latifolius 'Maki'

see pages 66, 67

  80-300 cm

Polyscias fruticosa
Ming aralia
see page 45

  100-200 cm

Rhapis excelsa
Lady palm
see page 68

   50-300 cm

Sansevieria trifasciata 'Laurentii'
Sansevieria zeylanica

see page 29

 50-120 cm

Schefflera actinophylla 'Amate'

Umbrella plant

see page 27

 150-400 cm

Schefflera arboricola

see page 14

 50-250 cm

Veitchia merrillii

Adonidia palm

see page 78

 150-800 cm

Washingtonia robusta

see page 64

 80-800 cm

Yucca elephantipes

see pages 41, 85

 70-500 cm

Yucca rostrata

see page 82

100-300 cm

Zamioculcas zamiifolia

see page 25

50-120 cm

Patio and conservatory plants

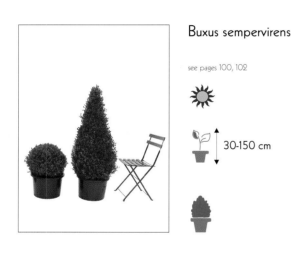

Buxus sempervirens

see pages 100, 102

30-150 cm

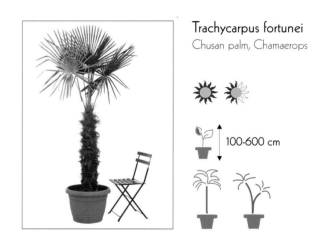

Trachycarpus fortunei
Chusan palm, Chamaerops

100-600 cm

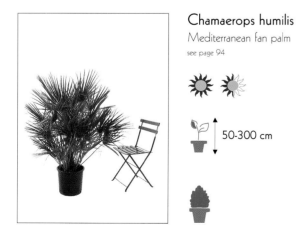

Chamaerops humilis
Mediterranean fan palm
see page 94

50-300 cm

Citrofortunella microcarpa
Calamondin
see pages 88, 89

50-250 cm

Laurus nobilis
Bay tree

30-300 cm

Metrosideros

see page 97

80-200 cm

Olea europaea
Olive tree

see pages 80, 97

50-400 cm

Pittosporum tobira 'Nanum'

see page 107

50-100 cm

Cacti and succulents

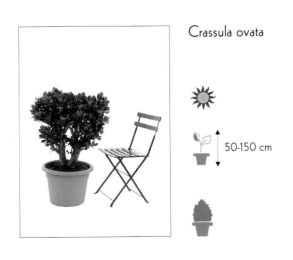

Crassula ovata

50-150 cm

Echinocactus grusonii

see page 56

30-100 cm

Euphorbia abyssinica

 70-200 cm

Pachycereus pringlei

see page 58

50-250 cm

Pachypodium lamerei
Madagascar palm

40-200 cm

Polaskia chichipe

see page 77

100-200 cm

Flowering plants

Aechmea
Urn bromelia

 80-100 cm

Anthurium
Flamingo plant
see page 32

 50-100 cm

Bougainvillea glabra
Paper plant

see pages 32

50-250 cm

Gardenia

30-100 cm

Guzmania

60-80 cm

Medinilla magnifica

see page 52

50-100 cm

Spathiphyllum 'Sensation'
Giant peace lily

100-150 cm

Strelitzia reginae
Bird of paradise

100-150 cm

THE AUTHORS ...

Sander Kroll began his career in garden and landscape architecture. In 1987, after completing his studies and working for several years in that field, he decided to turn his hand to the sale of tropical plants. Three years later, in 1990, he started his own company: Ki Plant International.

Joop Hüner began work at Ki Plant in 1998, bringing with him his experience in sales, and in the installation of large plants in national and international projects. Joop had also decided to make the transition to sales and marketing of large tropical plants after years of study and work in garden and landscape architecture.

Ki Plant International specialises in large plants and has become a prominent international exporter and service provider. Garden centres, interior plant specialists, and chain stores in various European countries are loyal clients. Ki Plant buys directly from growers in order to supply specified plants and to ensure quality. The company specialists are well qualified to advise clients on all aspects of large plants.

The publication of 'Plants, Extra Large' is an excellent example of this. Countless experts contributed to the inception of this book. It is the first time that a complete range of large plants in the living and working environment has been presented and illustrated. A valuable overview shows the enormous variety of plants available and just how they can enhance the ambience of the interior.

Ki Plant International Machineweg 302c 1187 NP Aalsmeer, the Netherlands Tel: **31 297 530111 Fax: **31 297 530101 E-mail: info@kiplant.com Internet: www.kiplant.com

MASCARENA LAGENICAULIS

THRINAX RADIATA   LIVISTONA CHINENSIS

INDEX

Latin Name	Common Name	Light	Available Height	Page
Pandanus utilis	Screw pine	ND	100-500cm	41, 65
Philodendron selloum		ND	80-200cm	26, 132
Phoenix canariensis	Canary date palm	ND	80-400cm	132
Phoenix roebelenii	Pygmy date palm	ND	80-400cm	10, 40, 73, 132
Podocarpus latifolius 'Maki'		ND	80-300cm	66, 67, 132
Polyscias fruticosa	Ming aralia	ND	100-200cm	45, 132
Rhapis excelsa	Lady palm	ND/S	50-300cm	68, 132
Sansevieria trifasciata 'Laurentii'	Mother-in-laws tongue	ND	50-120cm	29, 133
Sansevieria zeylanica	Mother-in-laws tongue	ND	50-120cm	133
Schefflera actinophylla 'Amate'	Umbrella plant	ND/S	150-400cm	27, 133
Schefflera arboricola		ND/S	50-250cm	14, 133
Tetrastigma voinierianum	Indoor grape vine	ND	100-200cm	31, 33
Thrinax radiata		DS	100-400cm	141
Veitchia merrillii	Adonidia palm	DS	150-800cm	78, 133
Washingtonia robusta		DS	80-800cm	64,133
Yucca elephantipes		ND/S	70-500cm	41, 85, 133
Yucca rostrata		ND	100-300cm	82, 83, 134
Zamioculcas zamiifolia		ND/S	50-120cm	25, 134

PATIO AND CONSERVATORY PLANTS

Latin Name	Common Name	Light	Available Height	Page
Buxus sempervirens	Boxwood	DS	30-150cm	100, 102, 103, 134
Chamaerops humilis	Mediterranean fan palm	DS/ND	50-300cm	94, 134
Citrofortunella microcarpa	Calamondin	DS	50-250cm	88, 89, 134
Ficus carica	Edible fig tree	DS	80-300cm	106
Laurus nobilis	Baytree	DS	30-300cm	135
Metrosideros		DS	80-200cm	97, 135
Murraya paniculata		DS	80-250cm	96
Olea europaea	Olive tree	DS	50-400 cm	80, 97, 135
Phyllostachys aurea	Yellow cane bamboo	DS	100-600cm	92
Pittosporum tobira 'Nanum'		DS	50-100cm	106, 107, 135
Trachycarpus fortunei	Chusan palm, Chamaerops	DS/ND	100-600cm	134

CACTI AND SUCCULENTS

Latin Name	Common Name	Light	Available Height	Page
Crassula ovata	Money tree	DS	50-150cm	135
Echinocactus grusonii		DS	30-100cm	56, 135
Euphorbia abyssinica		DS	70-200cm	136
Ferocactus townsendianus		DS	40-150cm	57
Pachycereus pringlei		DS	50-250cm	58, 59, 136
Pachypodium lamerei	Madagascar palm	DS	40-200cm	136
Polaskia chichipe		DS	100-200cm	77, 136

FLOWERING PLANTS

Latin Name	Common Name	Light	Available Height	Page
Aechmea	Urn plant	ND	80-100cm	136
Anthurium	Flamingo plant	ND	50-100cm	30, 32, 136
Bougainvillea glabra	Paper plant	DS	50-250cm	89, 98, 99, 136
Gardenia		DS	30-100cm	137
Guzmania		ND	60-80cm	137
Medinilla magnifica		ND	50-100cm	51, 137
Spathiphyllum 'Sensation'	Giant peace lily	ND/S	100-150cm	137
Strelitiza nicolai	Bird of paradise (white)	DS	100-500cm	76
Strelitzia reginae	Bird of paradise (orange)	DS	100-150cm	137

DS=Direct sunlight   ND=No direct sunlight   S=Shade

Original title: Plants, Extra Large — grote planten in het interieur…

Copyright © 1999 by Ki Plant Concept, Aalsmeer, the Netherlands
Text copyright © 1999 by Ki Plant Concept, Aalsmeer, the Netherlands
ISBN: 90-76710-01-5

First published in the Netherlands in 1999 by Ki Plant Concept

Plants, Extra Large - Decorative plants for the interior / Joop Hüner ; Sander Kroll
Medesign — Heemstede, The Netherlands, 2000

ISBN 90-76710-02-3

Copyright © 2000 for the English language edition: Ki Plant Concept
Ki Plant International, Aalsmeer, the Netherlands

Design and layout: Medesign — Heemstede, the Netherlands / Graphic design studio, specialist in graphic productions
with flowers and plants.
Art Director: Medinella Menger

Production, plant selection and organisation: Joop Hüner, Sander Kroll
Photography: Dolf Straatemeier
Photography (pages 115, 116, 117): Priska Ketterer
Photography ('A Thumbnail Guide' chapter and Florida (pages 117, 118)): Sander Kroll
Stylists: Frans Piek, Fred Zuidgeest
Illustrations (pages 114, 122, 123): Ronald Slabbers
Text: Adequaat communicatie-adviseurs, Marianne Rankin
Nomenclature verified by VKC — Aalsmeer, the Netherlands
Typesetting and lithography: Scan Studio - Heemstede, the Netherlands
Printer: NV Erasmus Drukkerij - Belgium
Publisher: Medesign - Heemstede, the Netherlands

Acknowledgements
Ki Plant International — Aalsmeer, the Netherlands
Urban Planters Ltd — Bradford, United Kingdom
Tim Smit, the Eden Project — St. Austell, United Kingdom

ISBN: 90-76710-02-3
Printed in Belgium